THE ENCYCLOPEDIA OF
PSYCHOACTIVE DRUGS

IN 25 VOLUMES
Each title on a specific drug or drug-related problem

ESCAPE FROM
ANXIETY & STRESS

THE ENCYCLOPEDIA OF PSYCHOACTIVE DRUGS

ESCAPE FROM ANXIETY & STRESS

TOM McLELLAN, Ph.D.

University of Pennsylvania

ALICIA BRAGG, M.A.

Philadelphia V.A. Hospital

JOHN CACCIOLA, M.A.

University of Pennsylvania

1986
CHELSEA HOUSE PUBLISHERS
NEW YORK
NEW HAVEN   PHILADELPHIA

SENIOR EDITOR: William P. Hansen
ASSOCIATE EDITORS: John Haney, Richard S. Mandell
CAPTIONS: Paula Edelson
EDITORIAL COORDINATOR: Karyn Gullen Browne
ART DIRECTOR: Susan Lusk
LAYOUT: Carol McDougall
ART ASSISTANTS: Victoria Tomaselli
                Noreen M. Lamb
PICTURE RESEARCH: Ian Ensign
COVER: "Woman Weeping" by Picasso, Bridgeman Art Library/Art Resource

First Printing

Library of Congress Cataloging-in-Publication Data
McLellan, Tom.
   Escape from anxiety & stress.
   (The Encyclopedia of psychoactive drugs)
   Bibliography: p.
   Includes index.
   Summary: Discusses causes and consequences of stress and the use and abuse
of drugs such as alcohol and marijuana in relation to stress.
   1. Drug abuse—Psychological aspects—Juvenile literature. 2. Alcoholics—
Psychology—Juvenile literature. 3. Stress (Psychology)—Juvenile literature. 4. An-
xiety—Juvenile literature. 5. Escape (Psychology)—Juvenile literature. [1. Drug
abuse—Psychological aspects. 2. Stress (Psychology) 3. Anxiety (Psychology)] I.
Bragg, Alicia. II. Title. III. Title: Escape from anxiety and stress. IV. Series.
RC564.M34   1986   616.86   85-31378

ISBN 0-87754-772-6

Chelsea House Publishers
Harold Steinberg, Chairman & Publisher
Susan Lusk, Vice President
A Division of Chelsea House Educational Communications, Inc.

133 Christopher Street, New York, NY 10014

345 Whitney Avenue, New Haven, CT 05510

5014 West Chester Pike, Edgemont, PA 19028

CONTENTS

Stress affects people of all ages. It can be debilitating and cause anxiety, depression, and physical symptoms such as a dry mouth and upset stomach, or be positive and stimulate the desire to achieve, in which case it is called "eustress," without which few things would be accomplished.

FOREWORD

In the Mainstream of American Life

The rapid growth of drug use and abuse is one of the most dramatic changes in the fabric of American society in the last 20 years. The United States has the highest level of psychoactive drug use of any industrialized society. It is 10 to 30 times greater than it was 20 years ago.

According to a recent Gallup poll, young people consider drugs the leading problem that they face. One of the legacies of the social upheaval of the 1960s is that psychoactive drugs have become part of the mainstream of American life. Schools, homes, and communities cannot be "drug proofed." There is a demand for drugs—and the supply is plentiful. Social norms have changed and drugs are not only available—they are everywhere.

Almost all drug use begins in the preteen and teenage years. These years are few in the total life cycle, but critical in the maturation process. During these years adolescents face the difficult tasks of discovering their identity, clarifying their sexual roles, asserting their independence, learning to cope with authority, and searching for goals that will give their lives meaning. During this intense period of growth, conflict is inevitable and the temptation to use drugs is great. Drugs are readily available, adolescents are curious and vulnerable, there is peer pressure to experiment, and there is the temptation to escape from conflicts.

No matter what their age or socioeconomic status, no group is immune to the allure and effects of psychoactive drugs. The U.S. Surgeon General's report, "Healthy People," indicates that 30% of all deaths in the United States

Alcohol and tobacco are the drugs most widely used by young Americans. This 1984 poster, incorporating lyrics from a song by The Police, a popular rock group, was released in Massachusetts as part of a state-wide effort to discourage young drivers from drinking.

are premature because of alcohol and tobacco use. However, the most shocking development in this report is that mortality in the age group between 15 and 24 has increased since 1960 despite the fact that death rates for all other age groups have declined in the 20th century. Accidents, suicides, and homicides are the leading cause of death in young people 15 to 24 years of age. In many cases the deaths are directly related to drug use.

THE ENCYCLOPEDIA OF PSYCHOACTIVE DRUGS answers the questions that young people are likely to ask about drugs, as well as those they might not think to ask, but should. Topics include: what it means to be intoxicated; how drugs affect mood; why people take drugs; who takes them; when they take them; and how much they take. They will learn what happens to a drug when it enters the body. They will learn what it means to get "hooked" and how it happens. They will learn how drugs affect their driving, their schoolwork, and those around them—their peers, their family, their friends, and their employers. They will learn what the signs are that indicate that a friend or a family member may have a drug problem and to identify four stages leading from drug use to drug abuse. Myths about drugs are dispelled.

National surveys indicate that students are eager for information about drugs and that they respond to it. Students not only need information about drugs—they want information. How they get it often proves crucial. Providing young people with accurate knowledge about drugs is one of the most critical aspects.

THE ENCYCLOPEDIA OF PSYCHOACTIVE DRUGS synthesizes the wealth of new information in this field and demystifies this complex and important subject. Each volume in the series is written by an expert in the field. Handsomely illustrated, this multi-volume series is geared for teenage readers. Young people will read these books, share them, talk about them, and make more informed decisions because of them.

Miriam Cohen., Ph.D.
Contributing Editor

In the late 1800s Vin Mariani was widely consumed in Europe and the United States. Described in this poster as a "French tonic wine" that "restores health and vitality," Vin Mariani contained cocaine.

INTRODUCTION

The Gift of Wizardry
Use and Abuse

JACK H. MENDELSON, M.D.
NANCY K. MELLO, PH.D.
Alcohol and Drug Abuse Research Center
Harvard Medical School—McLean Hospital

Dorothy to the Wizard:

"I think you are a very bad man," said Dorothy.
"Oh, no, my dear; I'm really a very good man; but I'm a very bad Wizard."
—from THE WIZARD OF OZ

Man is endowed with the gift of wizardry, a talent for discovery and invention. The discovery and invention of substances that change the way we feel and behave are among man's special accomplishments, and like so many other products of our wizardry, these substances have the capacity to harm as well as to help. The substance itself is neutral, an intricate molecular structure. Yet, "too much" can be sickening, even deadly. It is man who decides how each substance is used, and it is man's beliefs and perceptions that give this neutral substance the attributes to heal or destroy.

Consider alcohol—available to all and yet regarded with intense ambivalence from biblical times to the present day. The use of alcoholic beverages dates back to our earliest ancestors. Alcohol use and misuse became associated with the worship of gods and demons. One of the most powerful Greek gods was Dionysus, lord of fruitfulness and god of wine. The Romans adopted Dionysus but changed his name to Bacchus. Festivals and holidays associated with Bacchus celebrated the harvest and the origins of life. Time has blurred the images of the Bacchanalian festival, but the theme of drunkenness as a major part of celebration has survived the pagan gods and remains a familiar part of modern society. The term "Bacchanalian festival" conveys a more appealing image than "drunken orgy" or "pot

13

party," but whatever the label, some of the celebrants will inevitably start up the "high" escalator to the next plateau. Once there, the de-escalation is difficult for many.

According to reliable estimates, one out of every ten Americans develops a serious alcohol-related problem sometime in his or her lifetime. In addition, automobile accidents caused by drunken drivers claim the lives of tens of thousands every year. Many of the victims are gifted young people, just starting out in adult life. Hospital emergency rooms abound with patients seeking help for alcohol-related injuries.

Who is to blame? Can we blame the many manufacturers who produce such an amazing variety of alcoholic beverages? Should we blame the educators who fail to explain the perils of intoxication, or so exaggerate the dangers of drinking that no one could possibly believe them? Are friends to blame—those peers who urge others to "drink more and faster," or the macho types who stress the importance of being able to "hold your liquor"? Casting blame, however, is hardly constructive, and pointing the finger is a fruitless way to deal with problems. Alcoholism and drug abuse have few culprits but many victims. Accountability begins with each of us, every time we choose to use or to misuse an intoxicating substance.

It is ironic that some of man's earliest medicines, derived from natural plant products, are used today to poison and to intoxicate. Relief from pain and suffering is one of society's many continuing goals. Over 3,000 years ago, the Therapeutic Papyrus of Thebes, one of our earliest written records, gave instructions for the use of opium in the treatment of pain. Opium, in the form of its major derivative, morphine, remains one of the most powerful drugs we have for pain relief. But opium, morphine, and similar compounds, such as heroin, have also been used by many to induce changes in mood and feeling. Another example of man's misuse of a natural substance is the coca leaf, which for centuries was used by the Indians of Peru to reduce fatigue and hunger. Its modern derivative, cocaine, has important medical use as a local anesthetic. Unfortunately, its increasing abuse in the 1980s has reached epidemic proportions.

The purpose of this series is to provide information about the nature and behavioral effects of alcohol and drugs, and the probable consequences of both their moderate use and abuse. The authors believe that up-to-date, objective information about alcohol and drugs will help readers make better decisions as to whether to use them or not. The information presented here (and in other books in this series) is based on many clinical and laboratory studies and observations by people from diverse walks of life.

Over the centuries, novelists, poets, and dramatists have provided us with many insights into the beneficial and problematic aspects of alcohol and drug use. Physicians, lawyers, biologists, psychologists, and social scientists have contributed to a better understanding of the causes and consequences of using these substances. The authors in this series have attempted to gather and condense all the latest information about drug use and abuse. They have also described the sometimes wide gaps in our knowledge and have suggested some new ways to answer many difficult questions.

One such question, for example, is how do alcohol and drug problems get started? And what is the best way to treat them when they do? Not too many years ago, alcoholics and drug abusers were regarded as evil, immoral, or both. It is now recognized that these persons suffer from very complicated diseases involving deep psychological and social problems. To understand how the disease begins and progresses, it is necessary to understand the nature of the substance, the behavior of the afflicted person, and the characteristics of the society or culture in which he lives.

The diagram below shows the interaction of these three factors. The arrows indicate that the substance not only affects the user personally, but the society as well. Society influences attitudes towards the substance, which in turn affect its availability. The substance's impact upon the society may support or discourage the use and abuse of that substance.

SUBSTANCE
(ALCOHOL OR DRUG)

PERSON ⟷ SOCIETY

Thomas Edison, the inventor of the phonograph and the light bulb, was, along with such celebrities as the author Jules Verne, one of many people who endorsed cocaine-containing Vin Mariani at the turn of the century.

Although many of the social environments we live in are very similar, some of the most subtle differences can strongly influence our thinking and behavior. Where we live, go to school and work, whom we discuss things with—all influence our opinions about drug use and misuse. Yet we also share certain commonly accepted beliefs that outweigh any differences in our attitudes. The authors in this series have tried to identify and discuss the central, most crucial issues concerning drug use and misuse.

Regrettably, man's wizardry in developing new substances in medical therapeutics has not always been paralleled by intelligent usage. Although we do know a great deal about the effects of alcohol and drugs, we have yet to learn how to impart that knowledge, especially to young adults.

Does it matter? What harm does it do to smoke a little pot or have a few beers? What is it like to be intoxicated? How long does it last? Will it make me feel really fine? Will it make me sick? What are the risks? These are but a few of the questions answered in this series, which, hopefully, will enable the reader to make wise decisions concerning the crucial issue of drugs.

Information sensibly acted upon can go a long way towards helping everyone develop his or her best self. As one keen and sensitive observer, Dr. Lewis Thomas, has said,

> *"There is nothing at all absurd about the human condition. We matter. It seems to me a good guess, hazarded by a good many people who have thought about it, that we may be engaged in the formation of something like a mind for the life of this planet. If this is so, we are still at the most primitive stage, still fumbling with language and thinking, but infinitely capacitated for the future. Looked at this way, it is remarkable that we've come as far as we have in so short a period, really no time at all as geologists measure time. We are the newest, the youngest, and the brightest thing around."*

The movie Reefer Madness *is an example of the ineffectiveness of scare tactics. Produced in the 1930s to discourage marijuana use, the film exaggerated the drug's hazards, and is now viewed as a comedy.*

AUTHOR'S PREFACE

People most commonly use drugs or alcohol for recreational purposes because these substances are reputed to increase enjoyment or reduce the unpleasantness of a boring, lonesome, anxious, or otherwise stressful situation. In an effort to discourage recreational drug use, scare tactics emphasizing negative effects have frequently been used. Nevertheless, the simple facts are that most of the available drugs (including alcohol) do have very powerful effects on mood and under certain conditions can enhance the pleasure of good times and alleviate the discomfort of bad times.

This book was written not to scare, but to explore, honestly and intelligently, the facts about drug usage and stress—how drugs work, their immediate effects on the body, and their overall impact on the individual and society.

Specifically, three types of commonly available drugs—alcohol, marijuana, and the stimulants—will be examined, focusing on their effects, the biological and situational factors that influence the nature of these effects, and the reason these drugs make a person feel good, especially during periods of stress.

In order to better understand drugs and stress one must first understand the common emotional problems that often accompany stress and the nature of stress and its effects, both positive and negative, on the body, the mind, and particularly on the emotional state, or "mood." These subjects will be discussed, particularly stressing the importance of developing strategies for dealing with these effects.

Finally, the book looks at the effectiveness of drugs as stress-relievers. Data accumulated from ten years of research have shown that people who use available street drugs to "handle" or "get through" problems of anxiety, depression, loneliness, and boredom do indeed get some benefits from these drugs. However, these people also run the risk of developing a drug habit and chronic emotional problems, often the problems they originally used the drugs to avoid.

The facts presented here should make it possible for an individual to make an informed choice regarding the best strategy for handling the stress that is an unavoidable part of everyday life.

Stress is often a contributor to heart failure, the leading cause of death in the United States. This computer, which simulates cardiac arrest, trains medical students to respond swiftly and accurately.

CHAPTER 1

STRESS AND ITS CONSEQUENCES

*I*n our high-pressure, high-tech society, stress has become an everyday word. It is the topic of television talk shows and the primary focus of several kinds of psychotherapy. Stress-management workshops are popular on college campuses and among high-powered business executives. Throughout the nation, people young and old are seeking new strategies to cope with stress.

What Is Stress?

According to Dr. Hans Selye, a leading authority on the subject, stress is simply the "nonspecific response of the body to any demand." Stress is always present, accompanying every human activity, whether it be physical, intellectual, emotional, or social. The only time we are really free from stress is when we are dead.

In most cases the word "stress" conjures up a negative image. This is because stress is generally associated with "distress," a condition which ranges from being mildly unpleasant to extremely dangerous, causing such physical illnesses as headache, ulcers, and even heart disease.

All stress is not bad, however. Not only can it be positive but it can actually be curative. This type of stress, known as "eustress," serves as a stimulus to action, and without it little would get done in the world.

Stress Affects Everyone Differently

How people react to stress varies greatly. A situation that evokes a high level of stress in one person may barely elicit a response from another person.

An illustrative example is one's first dive from the high diving board. Recall how it felt to climb the ladder, step to the board's edge, leap into the air, and plunge into the water. The experience may have been exhilarating or terrifying, depending on who you are or perhaps even on what day it occurred. For one person it may be the inspiration for an Olympic diving career. For another person it may inspire only a fervent "never again." The act of diving is consistent, but for one the resulting stress is positive, a spur to accomplishment. For the other, the stress is excessive and negative, and becomes a deterrent to action.

The Many Forms of Stress

Whenever a physical or emotional demand is made of the body, it experiences stress. Any type of demand may cause either a physical and/or an emotional response. A physical response may include perspiration, the shakes, or even exhaustion.

Stress is most commonly perceived as an emotional

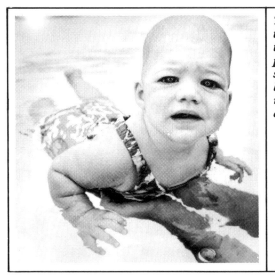

The babies pictured on this and the following page illustrate two types of responses to a new and potentially threatening situation—the first swimming lesson. This 7-month-old baby responded by displaying anxiety and apprehension.

response, however. Generally, one associates stress only with negative emotional responses, such as anxiety, tension, or depression, but positive emotional reactions, such as excitement or exhilaration, are also responses to certain types of stressful situations. Within the broad framework, most, if not all, emotions are stress reactions—that is, responses to the demands of everyday life.

Problems Demand Solutions

Situations that require solutions and thus create stress occur in all areas and at all times of life. In every one of the following examples, the individual experiences stress, though it may be perceived and acted upon in various ways.

One-year-old Jane wants to move from the hallway to the door.

Ten-year-old Bob discovers that the kid up the street took his bike after his parents told him never to let anyone ride it.

Sixteen-year-old Mary has two minutes to solve a difficult word problem on a math exam before the bell rings.

In analyzing situations such as these, one tends to put them into categories. Jane's problem is physical; Bob's is emotional; and Mary's is intellectual. However, the process

Unlike the baby shown on the previous page, this 10-month-old infant seems relaxed and, indeed, truly delighted by his first experience in a swimming pool.

that each of these individuals uses to solve his or her problem does, in fact, involve a combination of thought, emotion, and action.

It is easy to see that Jane's problem—that of getting from the hallway to the door—requires a physical response. Less obvious, however, is the intellectual response that must occur before any movement is possible. For mature individuals, the thought processes involved in moving from one place to another are so automatic that they occur without our being conscious of them. For a baby, however, the solution to the problem of locomotion is more complex. The infant may have to decide whether to crawl or to walk—an intellectual response. Furthermore, a baby is exhilarated by moving from hallway to door—an emotional response. And only after these responses does the infant actually move—a physical response.

The combined intellectual-emotional demands of the third type of problem are probably easier to recognize: "If a farmer picked one and one-half bushels of apples in three hours, how many bushels of apples . . . ?" Confronted with such a problem and given a limited amount of time in which to respond, different students will have different emotional stress responses. One may experience dread: "Oh, no! I hate

Infants line up for a baby-crawling contest in New Jersey. The ensuing race served as an early introduction to the stressful nature of competition, a facet of life that causes anxiety for people of all ages. The contest forced the babies to respond physically, emotionally, and even intellectually, for coupled with the exhilaration of competing was the struggle of deciding how to reach the finish line.

word problems! I never get them right!" While another will respond with: "Oh, I love word problems! They're so much fun!"

These emotional states may also be accompanied by a physical response. Dread often causes a queasy stomach, a dry mouth, or shortness of breath. Emotional excitement, on the other hand, is often characterized by deeper breathing, increased energy, or perhaps a fluttering stomach. Of course, the emotional and physical responses will also be partially governed by the student's intellectual ability to handle the problem, or even his or her perception of this ability.

The borrowed-bicycle problem is probably first experienced as an emotional one. Nevertheless, a good deal of intellectual and even physical effort may be necessary to solve the problem. The level of stress involved will depend upon the circumstances. If the friend who took the bicycle was unaware of the parents' rule, the solution might be a simple appeal to friendship and reason: "I'm sorry, but my parents told me not to let anyone ride it. Please give me back my bike." Some degree of mental and emotional discomfort is experienced, but it is probably minimal. If, on the other hand, the bike was taken with full knowledge of the rule and by the neighborhood bully, the level of stress will undoubtedly be great. The immediate response is emotional: fear, or maybe anger. Then follows the intellectual response: "How do I get the bike back?" Finally, there may be a tough physical response: Grab the bike and run!

An eight-year-old boy learns computer programing in a Dallas classroom. The widespread publicity regarding the necessity to own and understand computers has produced tension and anxiety in school administrators, educators, parents, and their children.

In the discussion of these problems, it is important to realize that each of the three aspects of our personality—intellectual, emotional, and physical—operates independently. They are delicately woven together to make up the human fabric.

Awareness of this interdependence is necessary when analyzing a problem. A situation that initially seems to evoke only an emotional response upon closer consideration will most likely reveal a physical element as well. For example, a condition of emotional stress, such as anxiety or depression, is almost always accompanied by a physical response, such as sleeplessness, loss of appetite, headache, and upset stomach.

Fine-Tuning Our Personality

Most likely, at some point in everyone's life a teacher has suggested that a good night's sleep and a good breakfast would help improve the quality of one's school work. This advice reflected the teacher's awareness of the relatedness of physical health to not only intellectual performance, but to emotional and social adjustment.

As a person passes from infancy into childhood, from childhood into adolescence, and from adolescence into adult-

Husband and wife cycle along the beach in San Diego. Physical activity such as bike riding is an effective way to relieve daily tension.

hood, he or she encounters new and ever more difficult problems. Human development is not a simple task. Change and growth are a lifelong process. As one matures, he or she becomes increasingly able to control this change and growth and, consequently, the responsibility for the development becomes increasingly one's own. This development takes place in the physical, intellectual, emotional, and social realms.

Because of the importance and interdependency of these realms there is the need to keep all the parts of the mind and body well balanced and in good working order, just as one would the parts of an automobile engine. A person must always strive to learn more, exercise as much as possible, study, sleep, and always try to get along with and respect other people.

This requires a lot of work, frequently too much. The mind and body work together to regulate how well a person takes care of him- or herself, and usually provide warning signals when the stress is too great. The response to excessive physical, intellectual, and/or emotional stimulation may be fatigue. Both the body and mind require time to adjust and adapt. Too many stress-producing situations can result in physical or emotional illness.

Millions of Chinese daily practice tai chi chuan, *an ancient martial art that is both rigorous and relaxing.*

During adolescence, physical changes, such as those that produce acne and awkwardness, are a source of anxiety.

CHAPTER 2

MAJOR CAUSES OF STRESS

*S*tressors, or the conditions that produce stress, generally fall into four categories: physical appearance and well-being; social situations and interpersonal relationships; school or job; and the family. Asked to analyze one's life, one would most likely be able to place his or her problems into one or more of these categories. The specific details may vary from person to person, but the general themes remain the same.

Physical Appearance and Well-Being

Throughout most people's lives, body image is a major concern. No matter what, one tends to perceive his or her body as imperfect. There is either too much here, not enough there, too little everywhere, or more than enough all over!

Adolescents are particularly sensitive about their physical appearance. This sensitivity concerning body image is part of the search for identity that characterizes adolescence. In addition, during this period increased production of hormones in the body causes many physical changes, such as the development of breasts and the growth of facial and genital hair. Appearance may reflect a desire to belong, to be like everyone else. Or, conversely, one's appearance may be used to express individuality or independence. No matter how a person chooses to appear—to him- or herself, to peers, or to adults—every decision regarding this image may cause stress.

Social Situations and Interpersonal Relationships

The development of sexual interest greatly contributes to adolescent stress. During this time dating begins, and the word "relationship" takes on a new meaning. Although one tries to be "cool," this new intimacy, while important, is also threatening.

Suddenly friendship takes on special significance, and the peer group becomes particularly powerful in determining what is acceptable and what is not acceptable. For most young people, having friends is crucial, and not having them can be a source of great unhappiness. In fact, to some adolescents, popularity is a measure of a person's value. The opinion and esteem of one's friends begins to carry as much, if not more, weight as those of one's parents. This can sometimes lead to open conflict at home. More often, however, the result is an internal struggle as one is faced with the problem of having to choose between what one wants to do and what one feels he or she is supposed to do.

Because of these pressures, social situations that are supposed to be fun—parties, dances, athletic events—can become a continuous stream of challenges related to one theme: social acceptance or rejection. "I wonder if she likes me?" "I wonder if *he* likes me?" "Should I ask her out?" "Should *I* ask *him* out?" "Will he notice me?" "What'll I do if no one talks to me?" "What if someone *does* talk to me?"

Nearly everyone eventually faces at least one of these questions. Whether one is relaxed or tense, popular or unpopular, social situations are stressful for nearly everyone. Part of growing up is learning to develop the skills to deal with this stress so that any social situation can be enjoyable.

School and Job

Two environments that are central to one's life and thus are major causes of stress are one's school and job. Because contemporary society emphasizes the importance of these areas, one's success or failure in them is often seen as a measure of a person's self-worth.

The school system, like society at large, rewards success, and penalizes, or at best ignores, failure. This highly competitive system is stressful for everyone, achiever and nonachiever alike. When a teacher uses the valedictorian as a role model, less successful students may feel so overwhelmed by their own lesser achievements that they are too discouraged to attempt to compete at all. In response to this stress, the student drops out, either physically and/or mentally.

The valedictorian's response to the competition is less readily apparent, but nonetheless real. The overachiever must deal with taunts such as "teacher's pet" and "egghead," or the barbed (and secretly envious) comment, "I suppose you got another 'A'." Perhaps worst of all, overachievers feel that they can never let up for a minute, that no matter what

Two students help each other solve a math problem in a Detroit classroom. Bussing, which transports children out of their residential areas for the sake of integration and to provide better education for the underprivileged, has caused tension and anxiety in many people, black and white, which has frequently led to violence.

the cost they must maintain the same high level of achievement, and that they must fulfill other people's expectations rather than their own.

The same type of competition continues in the work world. In most workplaces employees take note of who works hardest and who "goofs off," who deserves and gets rewards, and who gets rewards but does not deserve them. However, competition, like social relations, cannot—and should not—be avoided. Rather, here too a person must develop strategies and skills to handle the stress. This might mean channeling the stress into a search for a better under-

"Really boning up for the exam": To ease the tension during a biology test, the creative teacher placed this winterized skeleton at a desk.

standing of the whole situation, or it might include learning how to analyze a particular situation in order to determine how it could be changed to benefit everyone. The "distress" must be turned into "eustress"—stress must work for, rather than against, us.

Family Relationships

A person's relations with his or her family is particularly stressful during adolescence. Even the happiest and most secure home has an occasional conflict. The dispute might

Perhaps slightly exaggerated in its comic depiction of man versus machine, the Charlie Chaplin movie classic Modern Times *nevertheless makes an accurate statement of just how stressful our fast-paced society can be.*

be over something as seemingly unimportant as taking out the garbage. Sometimes, as adolescents try to assert their independence, the conflict is more serious. A seemingly innocuous question such as "When are you going to get your hair cut?" can be interpreted as a parental threat and an unfair interference in one's lifestyle. Often, parents are simply unaware, or unwilling to admit, that their child is growing up and is now better able to take care of him- or herself.

Another common source of family friction is sibling rivalry. While they jockey for first place in parents' hearts, children often reveal the stress they are experiencing through

A portrait, taken in the 1800s, of four generations of a single family. Until about 50 years ago, it was usual for all family members to live near each other, thus ensuring mutual emotional support. Today's shrinking family provides much less support during times of stress.

such remarks as: "Mom always did like you best." "How come he got more cake than I did?" "Why do I always get the hand-me-downs?" This competition often spills over into other areas of life. At school, for instance, the math teacher's innocent remark at roll call on the first day of class, "Mary Webster, Allison's sister? I sure hope you will be the same kind of model student she was," only serves to intensify the competition.

Of course, a family is much more than just a context for confrontations between family members. Even in families where the competition is the hottest, when the honor or safety of any member is challenged by an outsider, the

Franz Kafka (1883–1924), the Czech author of such fiction as **The Trial** *and* **The Castle.** *Kafka's writings, reflecting his own struggle with his frequently violent, unsympathetic father as well as with the world around him, often dealt with the stressful nature of family relationships and the individual's attempt to survive in modern society.*

family usually closes ranks. "I can fight with my sister, I can call her every name in the book, I can even slug it out with her, but don't let anyone else dare put her down, or they'll have to deal with me!"

Because the family is so important and the relationships within it are so closely intertwined, when a breakdown of the family unit occurs it is extremely stressful. The emotions brought out by such an event generally outweigh anything connected with sibling rivalries or clashes between parents and children. Marital separation or divorce, although sometimes necessary for the ultimate well-being of all family members, can have an immediate and a long-term distressing effect on everyone involved. Over time, family members

The parents of these children, who are in the playroom of a Chicago court building, are involved in divorce proceedings. Children often wrongly blame themselves for the problems of their parents.

usually learn to cope better with the stress of this major alteration in their lives, and over time the emotional upheaval subsides to some extent. However, during the initial period of adjustment, everyone involved is more vulnerable to the negative effects of everyday stress.

The most stressful situation for a family is the serious illness or death of a family member. To experience different emotions—anger, fear, guilt, sadness—is common during such times. Sometimes one imagines he or she is somehow responsible for the sickness that has befallen the other person. Or there is fear of being left behind, or anger at being abandoned. "What will I do without him?" "How could she go away and leave me all alone?" When a close family member dies, the stress is enormous. However, the passage of time and the process of grieving—talking about the loss, sharing feelings, recalling past memories—allow a person gradually to adjust to even this most stressful of events.

To explore the stresses of marriage and parenthood, these high school sociology students pretended that they were married and that the egg in the basket was their child.

The Henry Moore sculpture Family Group *(1945–1949) illustrates the importance of the family to each of its members, especially the infant, who depends physically and emotionally on his or her parents.*

CHAPTER 3

EARLY EMOTIONAL AND SOCIAL DEVELOPMENT

*H*ow one copes with stress depends on many factors. One of the most important is a person's childhood experiences. An infant's survival is entirely dependent upon the people who take care of it, and their importance to the infant's emotional and social growth cannot be overestimated.

From the moment the infant is held it begins to develop a strong emotional bond with its parents. The quality of this bond strongly affects a person's development, for throughout life it influences the way he or she will interact with the world.

The quality of the parental relationship greatly influences a child's sense of personal safety and emotional security. If the relationship is faulty, or if bonding never occurs, healthy growth may not take place. In such cases, children may develop distorted perceptions about themselves and the world. This can interfere with the establishment of normal relationships in adult life.

Almost all learning in the first years of life occurs within the context of the family. Parents and adult relatives encourage children to walk and talk and, by providing a rich variety of experiences, stimulate intellectual curiosity. It is with the guidance of these interested adults that the child learns about his or her internal and external world.

The World Inside Us

Not everything a person learns is gained directly from books, teachers, or dialogue with adults. Much more subtle interactions with parents and other close acquaintances strongly affect one's emotional development. Through these interactions one develops a self-image and a sense of self-worth.

Of course, these interactions can be positive or negative. Although they may never explicitly express it, parents may send a child the message, "You are good. You are loved." This knowledge helps build a secure personality and prepares a child to deal with life's problems. Unfortunately, and often unintentionally, the message communicated is, "You are bad. You are worthless." For the child absorbing this lesson, a sense of security and value may take years to develop. Or it may never develop at all.

The World Around Us

As children learn about their inner world and thus develop emotionally, they also grow socially and learn how to interact with the surrounding world. Here, too, the family is

Early school days can prove crucial, for they often mark the first time a child is separated from his or her parents for an extended period of time. Here, a child concentrates on stacking cylinders in a Montessori school, named for the noted Italian doctor Maria Montessori, a pioneer in early childhood education. The Montessori approach aims at developing in children a sense of independence and responsibility.

central to learning, and it is through family relationships that the child first learns how to relate to other people.

Early in a child's life, parents' perceptions dominate. The child, having limited experience in the world, quite naturally and unconsciously accepts these perceptions as his or her own. It is through parents' eyes that the child first sees relatives and other people and learns which parts of the world are safe and friendly, or hostile and dangerous. This is the start of a person's socialization, and it continues throughout life.

As a person matures, his or her horizons and experiences broaden. At first, social interaction is limited to one-on-one relationships with parents. Soon, however, social contacts usually expand to include siblings, grandparents, aunts, uncles, and cousins. Later, the people in the immediate neighborhood become a part of the picture. With entry into school, another social frontier is crossed. Relationships with peers develop—friendships (and enemies) may blossom. Finally, one comes into contact with the work world. And within all these relationships and environments one will always encounter varying degrees of stress.

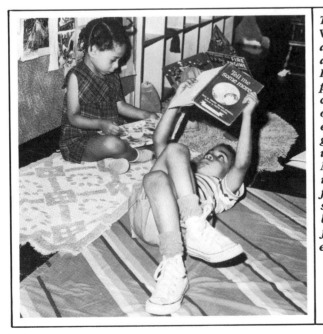

These two five-year-olds in Washington, D.C., are among the participants in a program known as Head Start, which provides underprivileged children with an opportunity for early education. One of the goals of the program, which grew out of Maria Montessori's work, is to instill children with a feeling of confidence and self-worth that could better prepare them for the tensions of everyday life.

The dreaded atom bomb. Although the nuclear age has provided numerous technological advantages, it has also created the nightmarish possibility of human annihilation, a major worldwide cause of stress.

CHAPTER 4

THE EMOTIONS OF STRESS

*T*here are many emotional responses to stressful situations. Stress disturbs one's equilibrium, and in an attempt to regain balance, the mind and body mobilize to adapt. The adaptive emotions experienced as a result of stress serve to warn, defend, and/or relieve. Though these emotions are often unpleasant, they are vital to the restoration of a person's normal state.

The emotions that are the result of stress fall into three basic categories: anxiety, depression, and anger. Anxiety is characterized by restlessness and is commonly described by words such as "tense," "jittery," "uptight," "nervous," and "panicky." Depression is manifested as a feeling of hopelessness; a depressed person may describe him- or herself as being sad, hopeless, down, or unhappy. Finally, anger may surface as frustration, irritability, hostility, or even violence.

Stress responses, however, do not usually occur individually. Thus, a stressful event may elicit any combination of emotions.

Anxiety

The feelings of uneasiness or apprehensiveness experienced in anticipation of a threatening situation (real or imagined) are commonly referred to as anxiety. A wide variety of situations will elicit anxiety. Competing with other people and studying for and taking tests tend to produce anxiety, as do new or unknown situations and conflicts with family and friends. Depending on many factors, including personality and mood, this response may range from vague worry to an overriding fear that something terrible—perhaps failure—is going to occur.

It is easy to understand how quarrels or other conflicts with family or friends can provoke anxiety. Such confrontations are often surrounded by a fear of physical and/or emotional injury. Though injury may rarely result, the fear is very real. Just as real is the threat to one's self-esteem: "Will this controversy show people that I am not smart enough, fast enough, attractive enough, or popular enough?" Such apprehension is a symptom of anxiety.

Anxiety is usually a warning that alerts a person to the fact that something is wrong and prepares him or her to face the anxiety-producing situation. A lack of anxiety may result in an "I-don't-care" attitude that, in fact, may increase the potential for failure. Moderate levels of anxiety, however, are beneficial. They supply motivation and added energy and increase one's ability to focus on the task at hand.

On the other hand, too much anxiety can be damaging, causing "hyped-up" and jittery feelings so intense that effective use of energies towards achieving a goal becomes impossible. Anxiety that persists for weeks or months at a time is a cause for concern. In such cases, a person may worry constantly and be unable to relax. Excessive perspiration or pounding of the heart may occur, as may difficulty in sleeping or concentrating. Although these symptoms are all associated with normal anxiety, their persistence over an extended period of time is an indication that anxiety is out of control. At that point anxiety is no longer serving as a warning, but has begun to control the individual, creating problems often unrelated to the original stressful situation.

Excessive anxiety may be caused by a number of factors. A person may just be overloaded. There may be too many important decisions to be made in too short a period of time, or too many stressful events may occur one after the other. Usually, when the crisis has passed, things return to normal. However, there are times when, regardless of external circumstances, anxiety continues. When this occurs it is important to seek parental or professional help.

Depression

Like anxiety, depression can be a protective response to certain stressors. However, unlike anxiety, depression is often experienced as a slowing down or a blunting of the effects of physical and/or emotional discomfort. Everyone has experienced depression at one time or another. Most likely, the feelings of depression followed some distressing event: the failure to achieve an important goal, rejection by a friend, the breakup of a relationship. The fundamental characteristic of depression is an unhappy mood, or "dysphoria."

Central to any discussion of depression is the concept of loss. The loss of relationships can occur through death, separation, or rejection; the loss of self-esteem through inability to live up to one's own standards or to achieve important goals; and the loss of full participation in the normal routine of life through illness, injury, or disability.

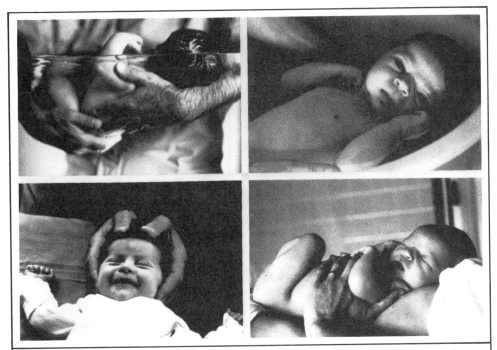

In order to lessen the trauma of birth, the French obstetrician Frederick LeBoyer developed a technique that includes the baby's immersion in warm water and that provides a more relaxed and less stressful entry into the world than do more conventional delivery procedures.

Losses such as these are frequently followed by a few hours or days of an unhappy or "down" feeling. Friends or relatives may be able to raise temporarily the sufferer's spirits, but depression usually resurfaces. Meals may be skipped and normally enjoyable situations may be avoided. Sleeping and concentration difficulties are not uncommon. Then, after dwelling on the problem for several days and perhaps talking about it with friends, the individual may gradually gain a new perspective on his or her loss. Life does not seem so hopeless—there are ways to rise above the loss, learn from what had been a depressing situation, and continue living. However, if the loss was very serious, such as the death of a parent, the healing process may take many weeks or months, if not years.

Depression can be triggered by stimuli other than loss. These can be physical, such as a biochemical change in the brain, or psychological, such as the presence of unresolved,

The sense of hopelessness and loss that results from unemployment, which in 1983 reached 9.5% in the United States, is a depressing reality for these men, who have just been laid off.

unconscious feelings. In addition, people sometimes become very depressed for no apparent reason. Experts have identified several factors that may make an individual prone to depression:

history of depression in close family members
neglect or abuse as a child
death of a parent during childhood or adolescence

Despite the seriousness of depression, it does tend to go away by itself, most often within a few days. There is some truth in the old cliché that "time heals all wounds." However, no one enjoys feeling depressed, even for a few days. Therefore, it is important to know that there are things that can be done to help get through the unavoidable low periods.

The single most important aid in overcoming depression is talking and being with other people. This is true even though people usually respond to depression by wanting to be alone. Though solitude may seem to be the most natural and easy response, it is probably the least effective way to combat depression.

Depression and anxiety frequently follow sudden loss, evident in this picture of a mother comforting her son after the family farm was auctioned off to pay debts. From 1983 to 1985, 14,242 farmers were driven out of business by financial problems, and 2,779 lost their farms, numbers rivaled only by those of the Great Depression.

Contact with others is helpful in several ways. By spending time with other people an individual learns that others care and may even have experienced similar difficulties. Friends, family, and even teachers may help the depressed individual see things in a more positive light. And sometimes just being with people helps. Going to a movie or taking a walk may divert one's attention from the depression and allow it to fade.

However, like anxiety, depression is sometimes more than a passing mood. When the mood persists for weeks or months, instead of just hours or days, it is called major depression, This condition generally is accompanied by several of the following additional symptoms:

> difficulty in sleeping *or* excessive sleeping
> low energy, tiredness, or fatigue
> poor appetite accompanied by weight loss *or*
>   increased appetite accompanied by weight gain
> feelings of guilt or unworthiness
> loss of interest or pleasure in usual activities
> difficulty in thinking or concentrating
> physical agitation and restlessness *or* lethargy
> thoughts of death or suicide

Of course everyone feels down some of the time. An individual may even be troubled periodically by a few of the symptoms of major depression. However, this does not mean that he or she is suffering from major depression. Such a serious case of major depression is set apart from normal unhappiness by the inability to shake off the low mood for weeks at a time, combined with the presence of several of the symptoms listed above. People suffering from major depression should seek professional help.

Anger

Any analysis of emotional responses to stress would be incomplete without a discussion of anger. Many of the same situations that cause anxiety or depression may also trigger feelings of anger. For instance, while students may experience anxiety the night before a final exam, it is not unusual for them to also feel anger, which is usually directed at the teacher who is giving the exam.

Anger often develops when an individual perceives something obstructing his or her movement or progress, or something frustrating the attainment of a goal. Anger may also develop in response to injustice, whether one is directly or indirectly suffering from the injustice. Though it is usually directed at someone else, anger can be directed inward, in which case it usually does not last long, and either dissipates quickly or becomes transformed into feelings of anxiety or depression.

The intensity of this emotion can range from mild annoyance to seething rage. As with all emotions, anger is experienced differently by different people. Some people anger easily and often, others hardly ever and only after great provocation. What is mildly irritating to one person may be justification for a fight to another.

A teenager, played by James Dean, grabs his passive, weak-willed father in a moment of anger in the 1956 movie Rebel Without a Cause. *Family conflicts are a source of stress and alienation for many youths.*

Anger can be released in many acceptable ways. It can be expressed outwardly and directly, such as by yelling or even threatening the offending party. Sometimes, however, it cannot be expressed directly. For example, if a student is reprimanded by a teacher, it may not be in his or her best interest to express anger directly to the teacher. What can be done to release this pent-up anger? "Talking out" the anger with someone who has a sympathetic ear can help. Or one may knowingly or unknowingly direct the anger onto someone or something that cannot strike back. The dog cannot fail its master in math!

There are other ways of expressing anger indirectly. Some people work off anger physically, such as by competing in sports. Sometimes, upon reexamination of the anger-producing situation, a person discovers that he or she had overreacted to something that would normally have been interpreted as nonthreatening. And finally—and in the long

A member of a street gang in the Bronx, New York, exposes his knife. Poverty, unemployment, poor housing, and broken homes are an understandable source of anger and frustration, which, when no alternative outlets are apparent, frequently surface as violence.

run this approach is sometimes the most productive—it is often possible to discuss the problem situation with the person who has caused the anger.

Violence is the one form of expression of anger that is rarely acceptable. People who consistently release their anger violently—hurting other people or destroying property—frequently have underlying psychological problems that may be traced to their childhood.

Some people, though not physically violent, may seem angry all the time. They seem hostile, always with a "chip on the shoulder." In fact, these people are probably experiencing significant feelings of depression and anxiety yet are only capable of expressing them as anger. Though these people are in great need of sympathy and understanding, their way of dealing with distress only serves to push others away and further distance them from better ways of resolving their problems.

A teenager takes a swing during a softball game. Athletic events not only provide physical exercise but are also a positive and healthy way to relieve tension and anger.

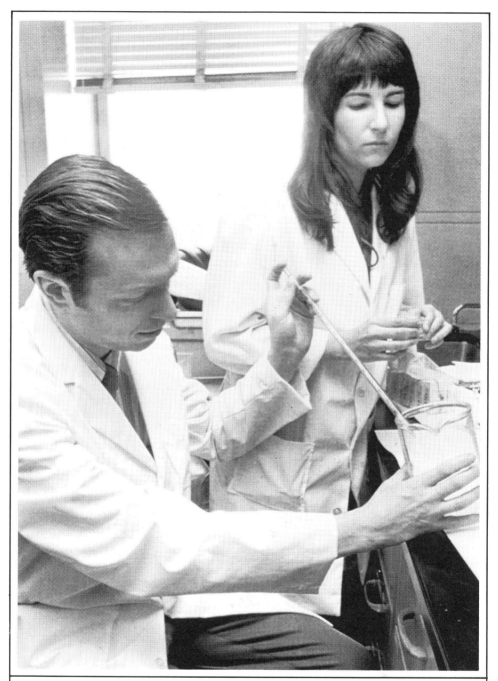

At Johns Hopkins University, Dr. Solomon H. Snyder and one of his assistants recently discovered the areas of the brain that are affected by narcotics. A better understanding of these areas could lead to a safe chemical treatment for heroin and cocaine addiction.

CHAPTER 5

DRUGS AND THE NERVOUS SYSTEM

*T*here are many different ways to deal with the emotional problems caused by stress. Unfortunately, many people, unwilling to take an effective but long-term approach, turn to the quick—but temporary—escape from stress provided by alcohol and drugs. While alcohol and drugs do sometimes provide temporary relief, they may also create more problems than they solve. To understand how drugs affect our minds and bodies, one must first understand the functioning of the nervous system.

How the Nervous System Works

The nervous system is a network of specialized tissues that controls the actions and reactions of the body, and enables it to adjust to changes in its environment. The nervous system, which consists of the brain, the spinal cord, and the nerves, is made up of billions of specialized cells called nerve cells. More than half of these are located in the brain.

The nerve cells carry information from every part of the body to the brain, which then processes this data and sends information back to the relevant areas of the body. Almost all of a person's movements, sensations, thoughts, and emotions are products of these activities of the nervous system.

To transfer information from one nerve cell to another, the body uses certain chemicals, called neurotransmitters.

These substances are released from the axon, or the end of a nerve cell, jump across the synapse, or gap, that exists between nerve cells, and bind, or attach, to the receptors of the next nerve cell. Depending on their chemical composition, neurotransmitters are excitatory (stimulating) or inhibitory (depressing). The type of neurotransmitter that is released, and the number and type of receptors to which it attaches, determine the actions and reactions of our minds and bodies.

Drugs, Alcohol, and the Nervous System

All the functions of the nervous system are dependent on the normal action of neurotransmitters. Drugs and alcohol, no matter how they are taken into the body, disrupt this action and alter the messages carried by the neurotransmitters.

Alcohol and drugs enhance, distort, or even eliminate normal information sent by the nerve cells that control the senses. This accounts for the enhanced sensations of color and sound associated with marijuana, the hallucinations associated with LSD and PCP, and the numbing and narcotic effects of opiates and barbiturates. These drugs also act on centers of the brain where moods and emotions are regulated. Thus they can produce feelings of well-being and euphoria, as well as feelings of paranoia, fear, and depression.

Like the naturally occurring neurotransmitters in the body, the active chemicals in psychoactive drugs are broken down into inactive forms through metabolism, the process by which substances are converted into compounds easily eliminated from the body. Because of metabolism, once drug use is terminated the effects of drugs gradually wear off and the nervous system soon returns to normal functioning.

However, if the body is regularly subjected to these chemicals, permanent changes may occur. For example, in response to regular disruption of normal nerve function due to drug use, the body may reduce or completely discontinue production of a natural neurotransmitter. Furthermore, the active chemicals in abused drugs may damage certain types of bodily tissue, particularly in the brain, producing a lesion, or dead spot, that cannot recover function. Finally, the body, forced to develop abnormal methods for breaking down these foreign chemicals, may become permanently unable to carry out normal metabolism of naturally occurring neurotransmitters.

Tolerance

Tolerance is the natural or developed ability of the body to adjust to the continued or increasing use of a drug. When tolerance develops, the intensity and duration of the effects of a given drug are less profound than when the drug was first used. Tolerance is both physiological and psychological. Physiologically, the nervous system adjusts to the continued presence of the drug. Psychologically, the individual becomes accustomed to the feelings produced by the drug, thus decreasing the user's perception of the drug's effects.

The phenomenon of tolerance creates a vicious circle of drug use. As the body and mind get used to the drug, it becomes neccessary to use greater quantities to reproduce the original effects. This, in turn, produces increased tolerance to the drug and a corresponding need for even higher doses. This endless cycle produces the repetitive need for the drug associated with addiction.

A major characteristic of tolerance is that it does not develop for all effects of the drug at the same time or at the same level of intake. Thus, it is possible for the positive, euphoric effects of a drug to be strong at low and infrequent doses, with relatively little sign of negative, or dysphoric, effects. However, as tolerance to the drug develops, and the dose needed to produce the desired effects increases, the probability of negative effects may grow disproportionately.

The Drug Experience

The perceived effects produced by any given drug are dependent on a great many factors. Particularly important is the quality of the drug, that is, the extent to which its chemical makeup is pure. Often drugs purchased on the street contain impurities, whose effects range from being nonexistent to being dangerous or even lethal. Equally important is the physical and mental state, as well as the recent history, of the user. Finally, there is the physical and social environment in which the drug is experienced. There are many confirmed reports of "contact highs" produced by what was thought to be marijuana but was later confirmed to be only a mixture of ordinary grass, weeds, oregano, and parsley. Similarly, there have been many reports of "bummers" by individuals who found themselves in stressful situations after taking what they erroneously believed was LSD, but was in fact merely some relatively innocuous substance.

Couples on a blind date make a toast to ease their anxiety. Alcohol's social facilitation effect—its ability to reduce social tension—is separate from its chemical effect on the body and more closely related to the familiar and comforting rituals surrounding its use.

CHAPTER 6

ALCOHOL

*A*lcohol is the product of the fermentation of naturally occuring sugars in fruits, grains, vegetables, and even flowers. Even when ingested in small doses it is toxic, or poisonous, to the body. Consumed in moderate to large quantities over extended periods of time, alcohol will seriously damage the heart, kidneys, stomach, and especially the liver.

Alcohol is probably the oldest man-made psychoactive, or mind-altering, substance. Despite its well-documented negative physical effects, alcohol has been almost universally used since the earliest of times to counteract unpleasant emotional states, to increase pleasure, and to promote sociability. The Psalms of the Old Testament sing of "wine that maketh glad the heart of man." And according to the ancient Greek poet Horace, "What wonders hath wine. It eases the anxious mind of its burden."

Alcohol and Social Tensions

Social gatherings are meant to be pleasurable and enjoyable, and yet frequently they are sources of anxiety. Most people at least occasionally experience feelings of inadequacy or uneasiness in a social situation. Who cannot recall that uncomfortable moment at a party, when, after being introduced to a new person, no particularly amusing or interesting conversation piece came to mind?

In these situations alcohol is used to ease social tension, which it does in several ways. The alcoholic drink, which is usually chilled, refreshes a palate dry from anxiety. Rather than being forced to stand awkwardly with hands in pockets or to shift restlessly from foot to foot, the drinker is also provided with something to do. And, since the majority of Americans do drink, participation in drinking customs emphasizes a common link between fellow party-goers. Thus these functions of alcohol ease tension and increase the possibilty of enjoying oneself.

This characteristic of alcohol to ease social tension is called the social facilitation effect of alcohol. It is separate from the chemical effect of alcohol, and is felt even *before* the alcohol is ingested. In many ways, the social context in which one drinks may even determine alcohol's overall effects on the body.

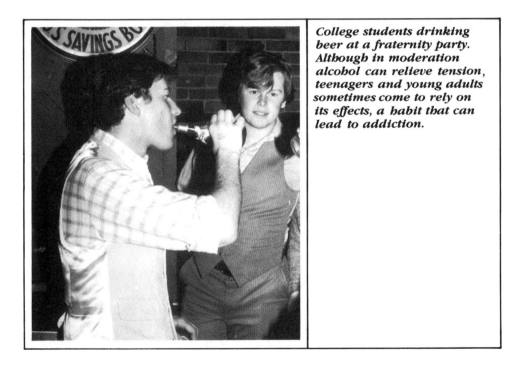

College students drinking beer at a fraternity party. Although in moderation alcohol can relieve tension, teenagers and young adults sometimes come to rely on its effects, a habit that can lead to addiction.

Because of the alcohol facilitation effect, the anxiety experienced in a social situation can be reduced merely by participating in the act of drinking and never consuming any alcohol. For example, problem drinkers who have given up alcohol often report that they feel left out at parties. However, many of these people have discovered that by joining the group but drinking only nonalcoholic beverages, they can enjoy the positive effects of drinking without suffering the negative physical consequences.

Pharmacologic Effects of Alcohol

It would be inaccurate to claim that the major mood-altering effects of alcohol are due only to the drinking environment. Clearly, if this were true, alcohol would not be used as widely as it is. In fact, alcohol has a number of pharmacologic properties that cause it to alter sensations, feelings, and abilities, regardless of the social setting.

Virtually all drugs have varied and increasingly stronger effects as they are used over a period of time and in greater doses. This is especially true for alcohol.

At social gatherings, alcohol can relax people not only by producing its physiological effects, but by providing a context for familiar rituals.

The dual nature of alcohol's effects has been known since alcohol was first used. Initially, alcohol is a stimulant and releaser of energy, but after time, and at larger doses, it acts as a strong depressant. One chemist, noting these contradictory characteristics, has called alcohol a "great deceiver."

Many studies have focused on alcohol's mood-changing qualities. The data are very clear. Using low doses of alcohol for short periods appears to liven spirits and produce greater happiness in normal people. Low doses also appear to reduce feelings of anxiety and depression in both normal and depressed people. High doses of alcohol, or moderate doses over longer periods, do not have mood-elevating effects on either of these groups of people. On the contrary, these higher doses can cause increased anxiety and depression in both normal and depressed people. Among alcoholics, the higher doses produce variable effects, none of them clearly positive.

Despite these findings, most people who use alcohol tend to remember only the light-use, low-dose, positive effects. They may recall how small amounts of alcohol helped lift their mood and relieve tension when a personal problem had made them depressed, frustrated, or insecure. Even heavy drinkers and alcoholics usually believe that using alcohol will raise their mood, decrease their anxiety, and improve their sleep.

These erroneous impressions have also been studied. Apparently, people in general, and heavy drinkers in particular, selectively remember the initial, low-dose, pleasant effects of alcohol and are generally less able to recall the later, high-dose, unpleasant effects. This phenomenon may be due to memory impairment caused by higher doses of alcohol, and is probably one of the reasons why heavy drinkers continue to abuse alcohol despite its adverse effects.

Tolerance

If alcohol is used frequently the body will develop a tolerance to it, and its positive effects against feelings of loneliness, anxiety, depression, and insecurity will diminish. On the other hand, alcohol's negative effects on mood, energy level, and sleep and its tendency to heighten feelings of anxiety will become more profound. Not only will alcohol become ineffective as a means of dealing with stress, it will actually produce or magnify the very symptoms of anxiety and depression the drinker was originally trying to escape.

Alcohol Abuse

Alcohol's positive effects occur only at low doses and generally only in appropriate social surroundings, such as at parties, other social events, and gatherings with fellow workers. This form of use is generally considered appropriate and responsible. In these situations, the positive effects of alcohol can be enjoyed and the negative effects minimized.

Most people initially use alcohol to enjoy the positive feelings associated with social drinking. However, many people later try to use alcohol as a tool to overcome emotional problems. Millions of people—including teenagers—throughout the world have suffered from alcohol abuse, which has led to addiction, physical disease, and/or psychological illness. Alcohol should never be thought of as a medicine or used as an escape from problems.

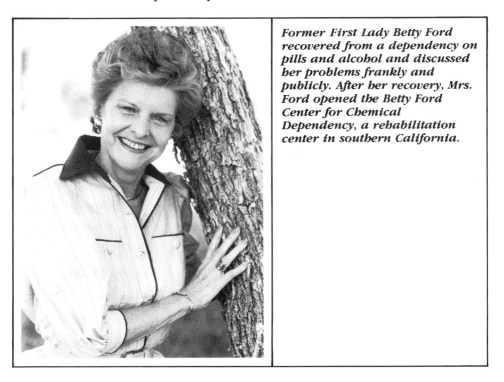

Former First Lady Betty Ford recovered from a dependency on pills and alcohol and discussed her problems frankly and publicly. After her recovery, Mrs. Ford opened the Betty Ford Center for Chemical Dependency, a rehabilitation center in southern California.

The Chinese characters for cannabis, the psychoactive marijuana plant. Use of marijuana goes back almost 5,000 years, to a time when the Chinese referred to the drug as the "liberator of sin."

CHAPTER 7

MARIJUANA

*M*arijuana, the common name for *Cannabis sativa* or *Cannabis indica*, is a plant that grows in virtually all climates and countries of the world. Cannabis contains hundreds of unique chemicals known as cannabinoids. Although at least 60 of these have intoxicating effects, the primary psychoactive component is Delta-9-THC, most often referred to as THC. Though THC can be ingested by smoking the plant's resins or by eating or smoking the dried leaves, most frequently the leaves are smoked in cigarettelike "joints." Inhaling the smoke brings both inactive agents, such as tars, carbon monoxide, and other particles, and psychoactive ingredients into the lungs, from which they are absorbed into the blood stream.

The "high" produced by marijuana is due to the actions of the cannabinoids on nerve receptors in the brain. Characteristic effects include the enhancement of sight, sound, and taste, a general feeling of relaxation, and the loss of tension. Because of these positive effects, marijuana is often used to assist relaxation and to enhance the enjoyment of already pleasurable activities, such as dancing, listening to music, or attending concerts. In addition, because of its sensory-stimulating effects, the drug is used by some individuals to heighten interest during repetitive or boring tasks.

As with other drugs, marijuana's effects depend on a variety of factors. Naturally, the size of the dose is very important: the larger the dose, the greater the effect. The environment in which marijuana is used also influences the nature and extent of its effects. Marijuana ingested in a relaxed, enjoyable atmosphere will often evoke pleasurable feelings. However, marijuana used in surroundings filled with hostility, tension, or fear will often only magnify these unpleasant emotions in the user.

Perhaps the most important factor in determining marijuana's effects is the previous drug history of the individual user. Frequent users develop tolerance, and therefore require more of the drug to produce the same intensity of effects previously experienced with lower doses. The phenomenon of marijuana tolerance has another, more disturbing, feature: the larger doses ingested by tolerant heavy users often produce frightening and undesired effects, experiences of which are sometimes called "bummers."

Who Uses Marijuana and Why?

Marijuana is the most commonly used illegal drug in the United States. More than 50 million Americans have used it at least once, and approximately 50% of all high-school seniors use it at least once per month.

National surveys have not been able to find any significant demographic, personality, or other background characteristics associated with marijuana users. That is, people who have tried marijuana are not particularly different from those who have not tried it. Furthermore, there is no longer the social stigma attached to those who have tried it.

There are, however, profound differences between the casual or one-time user and the regular user. These differences range from performance in school or work to overall satisfaction with life. In general, those who become regular users (defined as three or more times a week) begin using the drug earlier than those who become casual users (once a week or less). More than 30% of regular users reported that they started use before seventh grade. Regular users are also seven times more likely than casual users to be using additional illicit drugs, such as speed and/or barbituates. Among high school students, those who report regular use of marijuana have significantly poorer grades and are only half as likely to enter college or pursue other post-high school education as their casual or non-using peers. Finally, regular marijuana users who are not in high school have significantly lower incomes and report being less satisfied with their work than working people of the same age who do not use marijuana regularly.

It is important to ask whether marijuana serves the same function for the regular, daily user and the casual, infrequent user. Responding to a national survey, virtually all marijuana users, casual and regular, gave the same reasons for starting to smoke: "to feel good or get high" (95%), "to have a good time with my friends" (79%), and "because my friends urged me" (61%).

When casual users were asked about their current reasons for marijuana use, the first two answers—"to feel good" and "to have a good time"—still prevailed overwhelmingly.

John Nash, a lung cancer victim, was the first court-approved marijuana smoker in Texas. Legal arrangements were made for him to use the drug, which is helpful in relieving the nausea caused by chemotherapy, thereby decreasing the anxiety associated with the treatment.

In contrast, while regular marijuana users also continued to cite these two reasons, large numbers additionally responded, "to get away from my problems" (37%) or "to help me get through the day" (29%). Using marijuana as a means of escaping or coping with problems thus strongly distinguishes the regular daily user of marijuana from the casual user.

From these results one may be tempted to conclude that regular marijuana users simply have more frustrations and daily problems than casual users, and that marijuana, with its ability to intensify sensations, interest, and pleasure, is effective in relieving these pressures. However, the same survey asked high school seniors who were formerly daily users of marijuana why they stopped heavy use. The answers would seem to eliminate marijuana as an effective, long-term stress reliever. Of those questioned, 56% responded that they "weren't getting high anymore," 38% said they were "worried about physical effects," and 41% said they were "concerned about psychological changes," specifically loss of energy and motivation. Given these results, it is doubtful that marijuana is useful in alleviating the problems of boredom, depression, and tension commonly experienced by all people, and often especially by adolescents.

Those who continue to use the drug infrequently tend to report that even years later marijuana continues to produce the same positive effects it did during the first experience. In contrast, however, those individuals who use marijuana regularly to ease anxiety, tension, and depression became heavy users, though they generally experience a gradual decrease in the drug's effectiveness. For example, the shy student who finds that his or her initial nervousness at a party is relieved by marijuana may smoke *prior* to attending the next party; later, that student may even smoke prior to giving an oral report in class. However, though this strategy for relieving stress may work for a while, the fact that it does not work over the long term is evidenced by numerous studies. In fact, the daily users grow even more bored, have poorer and more incomplete educations, and are generally more dissatisfied with life than their nonsmoking peers.

That marijuana is at least partially responsible for the unsatisfying lives frequently reported by regular users is supported by the assertions of many former heavy users.

They often state they quit marijuana use because, instead of heightening sensation and increasing enjoyment, the daily, heavy use of the drug was instead decreasing their energy and enthusiasm. Ironically, although they were smoking more, they were enjoying the effects less. Thus, what seems at first like a good strategy for handling stress ultimately becomes ineffective and self-destructive.

Effects of Long-Term Use

In 1983 the National Academy of Sciences issued a comprehensive report on the positive and negative aspects of marijuana entitled *Marijuana and Health*. According to this report, there are many long-term physical effects of mari-

A chimpanzee puffing on a marijuana cigarette in an experiment conducted by the National Institutes of Health. The increasing use of marijuana led the United States government in 1977 to spend about $4 million on researching the effects of this drug.

juana use, but of particular interest here is the ironic fact that chronic marijuana use affects the heart and lungs in ways very similar to prolonged stress! The available data indicate that, just like physical and emotional stress, marijuana use increases the work of the heart by raising the heart rate and increasing blood pressure. Thus, the protracted use of the drug to release stress and tension actually has the opposite effect, at least on the heart and lungs.

The long-term effects of marijuana on mood and behavior are even more intriguing. First-time users almost universally report positive effects from the drug. However, 33% of regular users report that while intoxicated they sometimes experience such symptoms as acute panic, paranoia, hallucinations, and unpleasant perceptual distortions. Studies also show that "stable, well-adjusted, moderate users" report similar negative experiences from marijuana use.

The unpleasant emotional effects experienced by these moderate users may have resulted from stressful, threatening factors in the surroundings in which the marijuana was used. However, it is also likely that the bad experiences may have been the result of the increased dosage of the drug required by chronic marijuana users to obtain the desired high. This is a graphic illustration of what was mentioned earlier: tolerance to many of the pleasant effects of marijuana develops after prolonged use, and as increased amounts of the drug are used to duplicate the pleasant effects previously experienced, the risk of unpleasant effects increases.

There are numerous other significant emotional consequences associated with the chronic, long-term use of marijuana. Of these, one of the most serious is *acute brain syndrome*, a condition marked by perceptual distortions; sleep and memory problems; disorientation with regard to time and place; and the inability to concentrate or sustain attention to important stimuli in the environment. Acute brain syndrome requires hospital treatment and, fortunately, the symptoms seem to diminish and eventually disappear one or two months after discontinuation of marijuana use.

Amotivational syndrome is a less severe but more common condition seen in chronic marijuana users. It is characterized by symptoms such as apathy, loss of effectiveness, loss of ambition, and diminished ability to carry out plans. Amotivational syndrome occurs with varying degrees of severity in 30% to 60% of persons who have smoked marijuana regularly over a five-year period. Although amotivational syndrome is also seen in people who do not use drugs, there is clear evidence linking it to marijuana use.

Summary

The available data offer a conclusion on the use of marijuana to alleviate stress, provide stimulation, and intensify pleasure: marijuana may be temporarily effective for these purposes under certain conditions, but only when use is infrequent. Regular use reduces the drug's ability to produce favorable effects and, ironically, leads to increased stress on the heart and lungs, increased apathy and boredom, and increased risk of anxiety and panic attacks. Thus, what may appear to be a simple solution to the common problems of boredom, anxiety and depression may readily come to exaggerate the initial problems and produce new ones as well.

Filipino troopers in 1984 confiscated marijuana leaves that, according to authorities, were grown by rebels to finance a revolution to overthrow the regime of President Ferdinand Marcos.

A late 1890s advertisement for Coca-Cola. The claim that the beverage could relieve exhaustion had some basis until the 1920s Coke did, in fact, contain a small amount of the stimulant cocaine.

CHAPTER 8

STIMULANTS

*S*timulant drugs include amphetamine, cocaine, caffeine, and other preparations such as methylphenidate (Ritalin). These drugs have a general stimulating effect on the brain and body, and thus produce feelings of power, energy, and euphoria as well as heightened sensitivity to stimuli. Stimulant drugs may be taken in several forms. For example, most users of cocaine inhale, or "snort," the drug in white powder form. Amphetamine users may ingest the large dark pills known as "black beauties" or inject cooked or liquid forms of methamphetamine, or "speed."

Unlike many of the other commonly abused drugs, stimulants such as amphetamine and methamphetamine are often prescribed by physicians for medical problems. In particular, bithetamine and amphetamine, since they have a general appetite-suppressing quality, are widely prescribed as aids in losing weight. For many years amphetamine and methylphenidate have been used in the treatment of hyperactive children. These children have great difficulty attending to any fixed task and are often hyperactive and uncontrollable, especially in school. Although it may seem odd that a stimulant is used to reduce activity, in small doses these drugs have an action on the brain that improves attention and focuses energy, thereby reducing random activity.

It is this ability to increase attention, energy, and feelings of power and ability that has attracted attention to the stimulants during the past century. Sigmund Freud, the great physician and founder of psychoanalysis, studied and used cocaine for several years. In his early works written in the late 19th century he praised the stimulant action of the drug as a remedy for exhaustion and advocated its use to stimulate "clarity of thinking." At one point he recommended cocaine to a friend for easing pain; the friend rapidly became dependent on the drug, using as much as 1 gram a day (0.2 gm of cocaine being an average daily dose for today's user). Freud's description of his friend's "delirium"—extreme confusion and problems with attention—during heavy cocaine use is probably the first recorded case of cocaine psychosis. Freud dropped his earlier advocacy of cocaine use, stopped his personal use, and even published warnings about the drug. Despite this, many medical historians have accused

Sigmund Freud (1856–1939), the Austrian physician and father of psychoanalysis. Though in his early writing, most notably the book Über Coca, *Freud advocated the therapeutic use of cocaine, subsequent observations of the drug's dangers led him to publish warnings against its use. In fact, until recently these works contained the most definitive description of cocaine's psychological and physiological effects.*

Freud of unleashing the "third scourge of humanity," the other two being alcohol and opiates (heroin and morphine).

Who Uses Stimulants and Why?

Many people begin to use stimulants because they find that small doses make them feel stronger and more energetic, and at the same time calmer and more confident. Obviously, these effects have much appeal, particularly to students who "cram" for examinations, people who must work long hours or at more than one job, and athletes who wish to improve performance.

The stimulants' positive effects are even more attractive to people who are unable to concentrate, are normally unsure of themselves in performance situations, or who are suffering from mild symptoms of depression or low self-esteem. For people with these and similar problems, using stimulants makes them feel considerably more confident. At higher doses, these drugs produce sensory excitation and feelings of euphoria.

Development of Dependence

Negative reactions due to the use of stimulants generally develop in the same fashion as with other drugs. At first the user finds the drug useful in an ever-widening range of stressful situations and increases frequency of use. As frequency of use increases, the process of tolerance reduces the pleasurable effects of the drug at lower dosage levels. To duplicate the original positive effects, the individual increases the dosage, and the drug's unwanted side effects occur more frequently and become stronger. In fact, with the possible exception of alcohol, there is no class of drugs so dangerous.

Perhaps the most widespread and well-known side effect associated with the use of stimulants is the depression that occurs when regular drug use is discontinued. It is ironic that these drugs, which when taken regularly can be so effective in reducing depression, when discontinued produce such dramatic increases in that very same depressive condition. Perhaps most unfortunate is the fact that the most effective means of reversing the depressive state is through readministration of the drug. Thus begins the vicious circle of events that ends in drug dependence.

This withdrawal reaction—an increase in depressive symptoms—can occur even at low doses of the drug if the drug has been used regularly. Withdrawal symptoms include fatigue, lowered energy level, bodily pain, sleep problems, and a generalized deepening of the depressed state. These symptoms can last for as long as a week after a six-month period of regular use, and as long as a month following longer periods of use.

Stimulant Psychosis

Even more serious than the common symptom of post-use depression is the well-documented phenemenon known as stimulant psychosis. The major characteristic of stimulant psychosis is paranoia. As used here, this word goes far beyond its popular meaning of generalized suspiciousness or even unreasonable fear.

The paranoia associated with stimulant psychosis can be more accurately described as terror born of wild, irrational fears about people and places in the environment. To a person experiencing stimulant psychosis, a group of people waiting for a bus on a street corner may be seen with absolute certainty as a gang of terrorists waiting to attack. It is not an overstatement, nor is it meant as a scare tactic, to stress that stimulant psychosis can occur in almost any user of stimulant drugs under certain dosage conditions and in certain situations.

Toxic psychosis, as this condition is also called, is caused by the action of the stimulant drug on the nervous system. It usually occurs in individuals who have used abnormally high doses of a stimulant, or in individuals who, although not exceeding normal dosages, have used the drug with much greater frequency than usual—so-called binge use. (Psychotic behavior is also associated with heavy use of other classes of drugs, such as some of the tranquilizers [Quaaludes, Sopors], and with hallucinogenic drugs such as LSD, PCP, peyote, and mescaline.)

Psychotic episodes in response to heavy stimulant use are not confined to those few individuals with possible preexisting psychiatric problems or psychoses. Extensive studies have shown that the behavior produced by high doses of amphetamines or cocaine in volunteers with no prior history of stimulant use is virtually identical to the behavior seen in patients suffering from acute schizophrenia.

Even in less severe instances, episodes of stimulant psychosis are often accompanied by violence and injury. Perhaps most troubling, however, is the possibility raised by the results of the psychological testing of individuals who have had successive periods of heavy stimulant use. These tests indicate that in some cases the short-term, toxic states are not fully reversible. That is, some heavy, long-term users of stimulant drugs may never fully return to normal after an episode of stimulant psychosis.

Two celebrities who have had bad experiences with cocaine are comedian Richard Pryor, who was badly burned while "free-basing," and actress Linda Blair, arrested in 1979 for conspiring to possess cocaine.

A couple embraces in Washington, D.C., after completing a cross-country walk. Many hiking clubs across the United States promote their activities as a therapeutic means to relieve daily stress.

CHAPTER 9

ARE DRUGS USEFUL FOR HANDLING STRESS?

Stress is a natural consequence of living and can be either negative (distress) or positive (eustress). This book has concentrated generally on negative stress, and particularly on some of the emotional states that accompany it: anxiety, depression, and anger.

Everyone experiences these emotions in varying degrees and at various times, and it is important to develop strategies and skills to deal with them. One popular coping strategy, especially among people during their school years, is the use of street drugs and alcohol. The issue of whether or not drugs help one handle stress would be simple if it were possible to claim that alcohol and street drugs are not at all effective in dealing with the unpleasant emotions of stress. However, drugs do exert a powerful influence over negative emotional states, and thus can often provide quick relief from many of life's pressures. Less readily apparent, but equally true and perhaps more important, is that this relief is only temporary and carries with it some terrible risks.

Regular use of drugs at low-dosage levels leads to tolerance. Higher doses become necessary to produce the desired effects, but with the high doses comes the increased likelihood of unwanted side effects. In addition, chronic use at higher-dosage levels may produce more serious—and perhaps irreversible—physical and emotional problems.

Given these facts, why has drug use become such a popular way to handle stress-related problems?

It would seem that the major attraction of drug use as a strategy for handling stress lies in the fact that it is quick and easy. However, there are many other ways of handling stress, such as practicing a form of meditation or using biofeedback (both of which can provide profound relaxation as well as a sense of expanded consciousness and awareness), developing new interests, and performing vigorous physical exercise. These approaches require more energy, time, and patience than popping a pill or passing around a "joint." Indeed, some of these slower methods may even involve stress in their development. But their advantage is that they are safe and effective, not just for a few hours, but for a lifetime. Development of long-term strategies and skills for dealing with stress gives confidence and helps an individual achieve independence.

Four monks pass a statue of a recumbent Buddha in Japan. The historical Buddha reportedly became enlightened while meditating, a practice used today by many people to overcome anxiety and stress.

APPENDIX 1

STATE AGENCIES FOR THE PREVENTION AND TREATMENT OF DRUG ABUSE

ALABAMA
Department of Mental Health
Division of Mental Illness and
  Substance Abuse Community
  Programs
200 Interstate Park Drive
P.O. Box 3710
Montgomery, AL 36193
(205) 271-9253

ALASKA
Department of Health and Social
  Services
Office of Alcoholism and Drug
  Abuse
Pouch H-05-F
Juneau, AK 99811
(907) 586-6201

ARIZONA
Department of Health Services
Division of Behavioral Health
  Services
Bureau of Community Services
Alcohol Abuse and Alcoholism
  Section
2500 East Van Buren
Phoenix, AZ 85008
(602) 255-1238

Department of Health Services
Division of Behavioral Health
  Services
Bureau of Community Services
Drug Abuse Section
2500 East Van Buren
Phoenix, AZ 85008
(602) 255-1240

ARKANSAS
Department of Human Services
Office on Alcohol and Drug Abuse
  Prevention
1515 West 7th Avenue
Suite 310
Little Rock, AR 72202
(501) 371-2603

CALIFORNIA
Department of Alcohol and Drug
  Abuse
111 Capitol Mall
Sacramento, CA 95814
(916) 445-1940

COLORADO
Department of Health
Alcohol and Drug Abuse Division
4210 East 11th Avenue
Denver, CO 80220
(303) 320-6137

CONNECTICUT
Alcohol and Drug Abuse
  Commission
999 Asylum Avenue
3rd Floor
Hartford, CT 06105
(203) 566-4145

DELAWARE
Division of Mental Health
Bureau of Alcoholism and Drug
  Abuse
1901 North Dupont Highway
Newcastle, DE 19720
(302) 421-6101

DISTRICT OF COLUMBIA
Department of Human Services
Office of Health Planning and
  Development
601 Indiana Avenue, NW
Suite 500
Washington, D.C. 20004
(202) 724-5641

FLORIDA
Department of Health and
  Rehabilitative Services
Alcoholic Rehabilitation Program
1317 Winewood Boulevard
Room 187A
Tallahassee, FL 32301
(904) 488-0396

Department of Health and
  Rehabilitative Services
Drug Abuse Program
1317 Winewood Boulevard
Building 6, Room 155
Tallahassee, FL 32301
(904) 488-0900

GEORGIA
Department of Human Resources
Division of Mental Health and
  Mental Retardation
Alcohol and Drug Section
618 Ponce De Leon Avenue, NE
Atlanta, GA 30365-2101
(404) 894-4785

HAWAII
Department of Health
Mental Health Division
Alcohol and Drug Abuse Branch
1250 Punch Bowl Street
P.O. Box 3378
Honolulu, HI 96801
(808) 548-4280

IDAHO
Department of Health and Welfare
Bureau of Preventive Medicine
Substance Abuse Section
450 West State
Boise, ID 83720
(208) 334-4368

ILLINOIS
Department of Mental Health and
  Developmental Disabilities
Division of Alcoholism
160 North La Salle Street
Room 1500
Chicago, IL 60601
(312) 793-2907

Illinois Dangerous Drugs
  Commission
300 North State Street
Suite 1500
Chicago, IL 60610
(312) 822-9860

INDIANA
Department of Mental Health
Division of Addiction Services
429 North Pennsylvania Street
Indianapolis, IN 46204
(317) 232-7816

IOWA
Department of Substance Abuse
505 5th Avenue
Insurance Exchange Building
Suite 202
Des Moines, IA 50319
(515) 281-3641

KANSAS
Department of Social Rehabilitation
Alcohol and Drug Abuse Services
2700 West 6th Street
Biddle Building
Topeka, KS 66606
(913) 296-3925

KENTUCKY
Cabinet for Human Resources
Department of Health Services
Substance Abuse Branch
275 East Main Street
Frankfort, KY 40601
(502) 564-2880

LOUISIANA
Department of Health and Human
   Resources
Office of Mental Health and
   Substance Abuse
655 North 5th Street
P.O. Box 4049
Baton Rouge, LA 70821
(504) 342-2565

MAINE
Department of Human Services
Office of Alcoholism and Drug
   Abuse Prevention
Bureau of Rehabilitation
32 Winthrop Street
Augusta, ME 04330
(207) 289-2781

MARYLAND
Alcoholism Control Administration
201 West Preston Street
Fourth Floor
Baltimore, MD 21201
(301) 383-2977

State Health Department
Drug Abuse Administration
201 West Preston Street
Baltimore, MD 21201
(301) 383-3312

MASSACHUSETTS
Department of Public Health
Division of Alcoholism
755 Boylston Street
Sixth Floor
Boston, MA 02116
(617) 727-1960

Department of Public Health
Division of Drug Rehabilitation
600 Washington Street
Boston, MA 02114
(617) 727-8617

MICHIGAN
Department of Public Health
Office of Substance Abuse Services
3500 North Logan Street
P.O. Box 30035
Lansing, MI 48909
(517) 373-8603

MINNESOTA
Department of Public Welfare
Chemical Dependency Program
   Division
Centennial Building
658 Cedar Street
4th Floor
Saint Paul, MN 55155
(612) 296-4614

MISSISSIPPI
Department of Mental Health
Division of Alcohol and Drug Abuse
1102 Robert E. Lee Building
Jackson, MS 39201
(601) 359-1297

MISSOURI
Department of Mental Health
Division of Alcoholism and Drug
   Abuse
2002 Missouri Boulevard
P.O. Box 687
Jefferson City, MO 65102
(314) 751-4942

MONTANA
Department of Institutions
Alcohol and Drug Abuse Division
1539 11th Avenue
Helena, MT 59620
(406) 449-2827

NEBRASKA
Department of Public Institutions
Division of Alcoholism and Drug Abuse
801 West Van Dorn Street
P.O. Box 94728
Lincoln, NB 68509
(402) 471-2851, Ext. 415

NEVADA
Department of Human Resources
Bureau of Alcohol and Drug Abuse
505 East King Street
Carson City, NV 89710
(702) 885-4790

NEW HAMPSHIRE
Department of Health and Welfare
Office of Alcohol and Drug Abuse
  Prevention
Hazen Drive
Health and Welfare Building
Concord, NH 03301
(603) 271-4627

NEW JERSEY
Department of Health
Division of Alcoholism
129 East Hanover Street CN 362
Trenton, NJ 08625
(609) 292-8949

Department of Health
Division of Narcotic and Drug Abuse
  Control
129 East Hanover Street CN 362
Trenton, NJ 08625
(609) 292-8949

NEW MEXICO
Health and Environment Department
Behavioral Services Division
Substance Abuse Bureau
725 Saint Michaels Drive
P.O. Box 968
Santa Fe, NM 87503
(505) 984-0020, Ext. 304

NEW YORK
Division of Alcoholism and Alcohol
  Abuse
194 Washington Avenue
Albany, NY 12210
(518) 474-5417

Division of Substance Abuse
  Services
Executive Park South
Box 8200
Albany, NY 12203
(518) 457-7629

NORTH CAROLINA
Department of Human Resources
Division of Mental Health, Mental
  Retardation and Substance Abuse
  Services
Alcohol and Drug Abuse Services
325 North Salisbury Street
Albemarle Building
Raleigh, NC 27611
(919) 733-4670

NORTH DAKOTA
Department of Human Services
Division of Alcoholism and Drug
  Abuse
State Capitol Building
Bismarck, ND 58505
(701) 224-2767

OHIO
Department of Health
Division of Alcoholism
246 North High Street
P.O. Box 118
Columbus, OH 43216
(614) 466-3543

Department of Mental Health
Bureau of Drug Abuse
65 South Front Street
Columbus, OH 43215
(614) 466-9023

OKLAHOMA
Department of Mental Health
Alcohol and Drug Programs
4545 North Lincoln Boulevard
Suite 100 East Terrace
P.O. Box 53277
Oklahoma City, OK 73152
(405) 521-0044

OREGON
Department of Human Resources
Mental Health Division
Office of Programs for Alcohol and
  Drug Problems
2575 Bittern Street, NE
Salem, OR 97310
(503) 378-2163

PENNSYLVANIA
Department of Health
Office of Drug and Alcohol
  Programs
Commonwealth and Forster Avenues
Health and Welfare Building
P.O. Box 90
Harrisburg, PA 17108
(717) 787-9857

RHODE ISLAND
Department of Mental Health,
  Mental Retardation and Hospitals
Division of Substance Abuse
Substance Abuse Administration
  Building
Cranston, RI 02920
(401) 464-2091

SOUTH CAROLINA
Commission on Alcohol and Drug
  Abuse
3700 Forest Drive
Columbia, SC 29204
(803) 758-2521

SOUTH DAKOTA
Department of Health
Division of Alcohol and Drug Abuse
523 East Capitol, Joe Foss Building
Pierre, SD 57501
(605) 773-4806

TENNESSEE
Department of Mental Health and
  Mental Retardation
Alcohol and Drug Abuse Services
505 Deaderick Street
James K. Polk Building, Fourth Floor
Nashville, TN 37219
(615) 741-1921

TEXAS
Commission on Alcoholism
809 Sam Houston State Office Building
Austin, TX 78701
(512) 475-2577

Department of Community Affairs
Drug Abuse Prevention Division
2015 South Interstate Highway 35
P.O. Box 13166
Austin, TX 78711
(512) 443-4100

UTAH
Department of Social Services
Division of Alcoholism and Drugs
150 West North Temple
Suite 350
P.O. Box 2500
Salt Lake City, UT 84110
(801) 533-6532

VERMONT
Agency of Human Services
Department of Social and
  Rehabilitation Services
Alcohol and Drug Abuse Division
103 South Main Street
Waterbury, VT 05676
(802) 241-2170

VIRGINIA
Department of Mental Health and
Mental Retardation
Division of Substance Abuse
109 Governor Street
P.O. Box 1797
Richmond, VA 23214
(804) 786-5313

WASHINGTON
Department of Social and Health
Service
Bureau of Alcohol and Substance
Abuse
Office Building—44 W
Olympia, WA 98504
(206) 753-5866

WEST VIRGINIA
Department of Health
Office of Behavioral Health Services
Division on Alcoholism and Drug
Abuse
1800 Washington Street East
Building 3 Room 451
Charleston, WV 25305
(304) 348-2276

WISCONSIN
Department of Health and Social
Services
Division of Community Services
Bureau of Community Programs
Alcohol and Other Drug Abuse
Program Office
1 West Wilson Street
P.O. Box 7851
Madison, WI 53707
(608) 266-2717

WYOMING
Alcohol and Drug Abuse Programs
Hathaway Building
Cheyenne, WY 82002
(307) 777-7115, Ext. 7118

GUAM
Mental Health & Substance Abuse
Agency
P.O. Box 20999
Guam 96921

PUERTO RICO
Department of Addiction Control
Services
Alcohol Abuse Programs
P.O. Box B-Y Rio Piedras Station
Rio Piedras, PR 00928
(809) 763-5014

Department of Addiction Control
Services
Drug Abuse Programs
P.O. Box B-Y Rio Piedras Station
Rio Piedras, PR 00928
(809) 764-8140

VIRGIN ISLANDS
Division of Mental Health,
Alcoholism & Drug Dependency
Services
P.O. Box 7329
Saint Thomas, Virgin Islands 00801
(809) 774-7265

AMERICAN SAMOA
LBJ Tropical Medical Center
Department of Mental Health Clinic
Pago Pago, American Samoa 96799

TRUST TERRITORIES
Director of Health Services
Office of the High Commissioner
Saipan, Trust Territories 96950

Further Reading

Brecher, Edward M., and the Editors of *Consumer Reports.* *Licit and Illicit Drugs, The Consumer Union Report on Narcotics, Stimulants, Depressants, Inhalants, Hallucinogens, and Marijuana—including Caffeine, Nicotine, & Alcohol.* Mount Vernon, New York: Consumers Union, 1972.

Burns, David. *Feeling Good.* New York: William Morrow, 1980.

Deschin, Celia. *Teenager in a Drugged Society.* New York: Rosen Press, 1972.

Johnston, L.D., Bachman, J.G., and O'Malley, P.M., *1979 Highlights. Drugs and the Nation's High School Students. Five Year National Trends.* DHHS Publication No. (ADM) 81-930. Washington, D.C.: U.S. Government Printing Office, 1973.

Kandel, Denise. "Adolescent marijuana use: Role of parents and peers." *Science*, vol. 181 (1973): pp. 1067–1070.

Kandel, Denise and Faust, R. "Sequence and stages in patterns of adolescent drug use." *Archives of General Psychology*, vol. 32 (1975): pp. 923–932.

Selye, Hans. *The Stress of Life.* New York: McGraw Hill, 1976.

Relman, Arnold S., ed. *Marijuana and Health.* Washington, D.C.: National Academy Press, 1982.

Varma, V. P. *Stresses in Children.* New York: Crane, Russak, 1973.

Glossary

acute brain syndrome a condition resulting from chronic, long-term use of marijuana and characterized by perceptual distortions; sleep and memory problems; disorientation with regard to time and place; and an inability to concentrate on important stimuli in the environment

addiction a condition caused by repeated drug use, characterized by a compulsive urge to continue using the drug, a tendency to increase the dosage, and physiological and/or psychological dependence

amotivational syndrome a condition associated with chronic marijuana users and characterized by apathy, loss of ambition and effectiveness, and diminished ability to carry out plans

amphetamine a drug that stimulates the nervous system; generally used as a mood elevator, energizer, antidepressant, and appetite depressant

anxiety an emotional state caused by uncertainty, apprehension, fear, and/or dread that produces such symptoms as sweating, agitation, and increased blood pressure and heart rate

axon the part of a neuron along which the nerve impulse travels away from the cell body

barbiturate a drug that causes depression of the central nervous system; generally used to reduce anxiety or to induce euphoria

caffeine trimethylxanthine; a central nervous system stimulant found in coffee, tea, cocoa, various soft drinks, and often in combination with other drugs to enhance their effects

cocaine the primary psychoactive ingredient in the coca plant and a behavioral stimulant

dendrite the hairlike structure which protrudes from the neural cell body on which receptor sites are located

depression a sometimes overwhelming emotional state characterized by feelings of inadequacy and hopelessness and accompanied by a decrease in physical and psychological activity

dysphoria the fundamental characteristic of depression; opposite to euphoria *drug* any substance—plant, powder, solid, fluid, or gas—that when ingested, injected, sniffed, inhaled, or absorbed from the skin affects bodily functions

euphoria a mental high characterized by a sense of well-being

eustress positive stress which is pleasant or curative and serves as a stimulus to action

fermentation a chemical process by which yeast consumes sugars, such as those in fruits, and produces effervescence and alcohol

hallucination a sensory impression that has no basis in external stimulation

heroin a semisynthetic opiate produced by a chemical modification of morphine

lesion an abnormal and usually permanent change in the structure of a bodily organ due to injury or disease; specifically, a dead spot in the brain sometimes caused by drugs such as alcohol

LSD lysergic acid diethylamide; a hallucinogen derived from a fungus that grows on rye or from morning-glory seeds

marijuana the leaves, flowers, buds, and/or branches of the hemp plant *Cannabis sativa* or *Cannabis indica* that contain cannabinoids, a group of intoxicating drugs

mescaline a hallucinogenic drug found in certain cacti, chemically similar to amphetamine

metabolism the chemical changes in the living cell by which energy is provided for the vital processes and activities and by which new material is assimilated to repair cell structures; or, the process that uses enzymes to convert one substance into compounds that can be easily eliminated from the body

methamphetamine a popular form of amphetamine frequently ingested intravenously

methylphenidate a drug mainly used to treat hyperactive children; commonly known by its trade name, Ritalin

morphine the principal psychoactive ingredient of opium which produces sleep or a state of stupor; the standard against which all morphine-like drugs are compared

neurotransmitter a chemical, such as ACh, that travels from the axon of one neuron, across the synaptic gap, and to the receptor site on the dendrite of an adjacent neuron, thus allowing communication between neural cells

opiates   compounds from the milky juice of the poppy plant *Papaver somniferum*, including opium, morphine, codeine, and their derivatives, such as heroin

paranoia   a mental condition characterized by extreme suspiciousness, fear, delusions, and in extreme cases hallucinations

PCP   phencyclidine; a drug first used as an anesthetic but later discontinued because of its adverse side effects; today abused for its stimulant, depressant, and/or hallucinogenic effects

peyote   a cactus that contains mescaline, a hallucinogenic drug, and is used legally by certain American Indians for religious and medical purposes

physical dependence   an adaptation of the body to the presence of a drug such that its absence produces withdrawal symptoms

psychological dependence   a condition in which the drug user craves a drug to maintain a sense of well-being and feels discomfort when deprived of it

psychotherapy   a treatment of mental or emotional disorders or maladjustments using psychological methods

psychoactive   altering mood and/or behavior

receptor site   a specialized area located on a dendrite which, when bound by a sufficient number of neurotransmitter molecules, produces an electrical charge

schizophrenia   a chronic psychotic disorder with predominant symptoms such as paranoia, delusions, and hallucinations

stimulant   any drug that increases behavioral activity

stimulant psychosis   toxic psychosis; a condition caused by the action of a high dose of a stimulant on the nervous system, characterized by extreme paranoia, and often accompanied by violence and injury; this condition is sometimes irreversible

stress   the nonspecific response of the body to any intellectual, emotional, and/or physical demand

stressor   any condition that causes stress

synapse   the gap between the axon and dendrite of two adjacent neurons in which neurotransmitters travel

THC   tetra-hydrocannabinol; the psychoactive ingredient

in marijuana

tolerance　a decrease of susceptibility to the effects of a drug due to its continued administration, resulting in the user's need to increase the drug dosage in order to achieve the effects experienced previously

toxin　any substance that causes temporary or permanent damage to cells or organ systems of the body

tranquilizer　a drug that has calming, relaxing effects

withdrawal　the physiological and psychological effects of discontinued usage of a drug

Index